a
thousand
yellow
leaves

a
thousand
yellow
leaves

Marie Groundwater

marie groundwater

Lenore Langs

lenore langs

Dorothy Mahoney

dorothy mahoney

Karen P. Ouellette

karen p. ouellette

Leila Pepper

leila pepper

To my dear Elsie
with love
Danny

About the illustrations: The illustrations were chosen by David Pepper and taken from 19th and early 20th century Japanese woodblock-printed books by Isai, Hokusai and other artists.

Haikus are by Leila Pepper.

National Library of Canada Cataloguing in Publication Data

A thousand yellow leaves / Marie Groundwater ... [et al.].

Poems.
ISBN 1-894668-15-4

1. Canadian poetry (English)—Women authors. 2. Canadian poetry (English)—20th century. I. Groundwater, Marie

PS8283.W6T484 2004   C811'.540809287   C2003-905751-8

Contents

"It is in order to really see, to see even deeper, ever more intensely, hence to be fully aware and alive, that I write what the Chinese call The Ten Thousand Things around me. Writing is the discipline by which I constantly rediscover the world. I have learned that what I have not written about, I have never really seen, and that when I start writing about an ordinary thing, I realize how extraordinary it is, sheer miracle."

from Frederick Franck, *The Zen of Seeing*.

Gathering autumn,
in the darkening garden
the bronze lantern glows

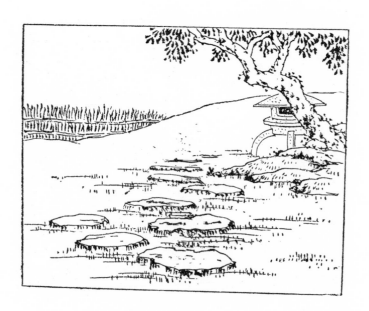

1

Spring Air

I could smell spring today
and my lungs hurt to breathe more deeply,
expanding with the lighter air,
my nostrils filling with the life and death of it.
Old Indian Creek came back
where we crouched to watch the
bubble throated bullfrogs leaping
easily from our reach.
Our sneakers soaked with pond scum
we squelched home,
happy with peepers in pails.
The Oak Wood came back
still sodden with last year's decay;
a narrow slit in the earth yielded up
garter snakes, one after another,
still sleepy as we pulled them
prematurely from their tomb.
We laid them in the grass,
watching their slow writhings,
tongues flicking like ferny tendrils
tasting the air,
tasting their recall to life.

I could smell spring today,
the life and death of it.

—*Marie Groundwater*

3

Capricorn

My mother never told me
What the sky was like
The day that I was born

Guelph in mid-January
May have meant lowering skies
Menacing clouds bulging
To deliver a blizzard

Or perhaps
It was one of those eye-squinting days
With sun so bright
The snow reflects
Silver sequins
And every sound in the clear cold
Is sharp
As a first cry

The baby I see in the picture
Looks quizzical
As though she can't yet forecast
The weather

—*Lenore Langs*

Dragon Eyes

she says we must buy a pound
there is no buying just a handful
of longan fruit
like lychees, a pimpled peel of yellow-brown
we consent
she smirks handing us the bag
warns us not to eat the seed
spit it out she repeats *spit it out*
while further down the street
a happy-faced dragon of red and orange paper
parades tall
two pairs of shoed-legs propel him
over the crowd
someone is banging a gong
he disappears into a restaurant
we get on a bus
consider the vendor's warning
as we open the dragon eyes
study the translucent whites
like peeled grapes
pop them into our mouths
spitting the black pits into our palms
we hold them
like black beads to worry
like dice we plan to shake
roll them into the street
as we leave
willing to be blessed
by good fortune

—*Dorothy Mahoney*

Elixir

the season lengthens
leaves are limp
and grass is brittle
while cicadas shrill
insistence on succession
will not surrender
to silence
though the hardened ground
will resist the seeded grub

nights soothe cool
and the moon grows full
there is talk of snow
in the mountains
and barefooted men
are building roads
with pickaxes
while emperors sleep
untouched in ancient tombs

in drought the great archer
shot the nine suns
like ducks from the sky
but lost the elixir
of immortality
his wife
forsaken to the moon

if emperors could rise again
like new moons
from desiccated shells
to call their concubines
and relinquish music
from buried bells of bronze
men would still swing pickaxes
and snow would tell on distant mountains
how bitter are
tea leaves left too long unpicked

—Dorothy Mahoney

After Eye Surgery

Under the patched eye
I see
projected on the retina
pulsing lumps of pink
moving slow tentacles
veined with black
like sea shrimp
Concentrating on them
for amazing seconds
I am looking inward to
the convoluted brain
As a skywatcher might view
through his telescope
an uncharted galaxy
I gaze into the depths
of my own mind
Below gauzy filaments
images lurk
faces that change shape
waver   melt into fields
that turn to forests
then become caravans snaking
from shadow to shadow
This imaginary landscape
in the realm of my brain
confounds me
I know each cell
contains a universe   but
in this other universe
what infinitesimal part
is *me*?

—*Leila Pepper*

8

To Witches

I own no cape   no broom
or pointed hat
but I am old
and have a cat
he is my friend
my confidante and guide
we spend our days together
and at night
he warms my feet
or cuddles at my side

O we will never know
how many ancient women
were forced in flames to die
whose only crime was being
as foolish-fond as I

—*Leila Pepper*

9

Pearl Cream

on my dresser sits a small jar
of "Ballet" (higher PEARL cream)
the lid ringed in two bands of gold
five Chinese symbols jeté in short spurts
like the ink we would push across paper
with straws during art class
the gnarled limbs of stunted trees
waiting to dry
waiting the blossoms of pink paint
just as I wait the promised renewal
the boxed assurance
"keep your skin lubricious snow white"
the cream made from *"precious*
Taihu Lake pearl and natural essence"
no other ingredients listed
"it can prevent our skin
from getting coarse and senile"
outside my window the snow is
crisscrossed by the shadow of tree branches
it will be another month before buds
become apparent

the jar will be empty then

—*Dorothy Mahoney*

On Listening to Mahler's Ninth

The composer never heard it performed
Died before Walter premiered
This saga of life's
Sadness and violence
Its moments of celebration

Bruno Walter conducted the Ninth again
In Austria
In 1938
Then fled with the other musicians
From Vienna
To America

We listen motionless
In Detroit's Orchestra Hall
No candy wrappers rustling
No clearing of throats
As the music moves through
Life's phases
Towards its ending
The final movement
Stilling down
To silence

—*Lenore Langs*

Seeking Neutrinos

The boatman
Who ferried his charges
Across the Styx
Held his lantern high
Illuminating that subterranean river.

Today, on this underground Japanese lake
The passengers paddle
A rubber dinghy
With no one to guide them.

Their shadows ripple behind them
As they inspect the rows
Of photomultiplier tubes
Fastened to the walls
Beneath the surface
Of the water.
They wipe the sweat
That sheens their faces
As air conditioners hold at bay
The fierce heat
From the earth's core.

They seek
Not Hades
But the far reaches
Of atomic space.

The lake's distilled waters
Are pure
As a shriven soul.

—*Lenore Langs*

Finally the Rain

Late September
and the ground is baked hard
far too early brown leaves
curl and fall
cover the parched earth
rustle crisply under foot
bushes wilt
flowers droop and die
tree branches hang limp and thirsty
this is desert land
a plague has come upon us
the whole world is dust-dry tonight
a fresh wind rises
and finally rain comes
softly at first   scattered drops
then in torrents   shining sheets
making bright puddles
under every street lamp
but this is temporary reprieve
we need forty days
of unremitting rain
the steady pounding of Noah's flood
to save this stricken land

perhaps in me too
the terrible drought is ending
at 4 a.m. words flow
rain down   splash the page
as I write again

—*Leila Pepper*

Lady of the Desert

A revelation –
painted on ceilings,
floors and ascending walls
echoing
the thrum of prayer...

At the looming-white mission
of San Xavier Del Bac
I walk with God,
my spiritual heart
catching hues & gilded images
through the small eye
of a tourist's camera.

Past great mesquite doors
and rows of holy relics
the radiant form
of a Madonna waits –
tiaraed in lace,
yearning to celebrate
   to dance her festive hymns;
and I can hear
the swish of her bright
Spanish gown...

I think of my mother
waiting home,
the Mary Day parades of youth
where a pale-blue Madonna
passed by –
the folds of her gown
stilled like lost wind,
lashes lowered in prayer...

On these ancient grounds
I am ready to laugh loud –
to dance up life
with old saints, the hem
of my wide red skirt
swirling wild
to the hallowed beat
of a desert guitar.

—*Karen P. Ouellette*

Centre Work

Finally I can move to centre;
after all the muscles
(the life knots)
are absolved from tedious
barre work –
the Cecchetti code
of legs controlled long
where beats are timed,
arms lengthened,
my marionette head
lifting the spine
one more inch,

I taste the salt
of pure exhaustion
where skin and bones
ache silent –
toes bleed warm.

Here in the middle of things
my pulled-back hair
flying free,
I dance untethered
from teacher
and fixed *barre* –
the hard-oak floor,
my heart strumming
a sweeter tune

– a musical shift
where every dulcet string,
every worked out part
lightens; lifts high
like breeze
until I become air and spirit
leaping

—*Karen P. Ouellette*

From my garden now
swords of blue iris point up;
Spring dares me outside

She Never Finished Anything

was distracted from her prayers
by the flash of a finch's wing
decided to follow a regime
of monday cleaning tuesday laundry
but took her coffee
to the back yard for ten minutes
on the first monday
and stayed all morning
watching the light change
on the leaves of the lilac

she started to tuck away money for a rainy day
but decided jamaica qualified
had every intention of finishing her novel
but found ten-line poems quicker
would have been
organized, efficient, productive
but life kept
distracting her

—*Lenore Langs*

In City Streets

In city streets the fields persist
with iron and stubborn will
By fences in lawns uncut
dandelions and night-shade thrive
There is a feeling here   that
left unended for a little while
those fields would soon encroach
spring up in jungle growth
profuse and wilful   to undermine
foundations   stony sills   and walls
push up an army of alien shoots
to root and tangle and entwine
A conquest so complete
explorers centuries from now
digging this mound would view
with puzzled eyes   our artifacts
I hurry hurry home
make fast the door   then
listen apprehensively until I catch
the comfort of a mower   as it trims
to neat conformity the forward field

—*Leila Pepper*

Dirt

I love a load of dirt
dropped into the yard
from elsewhere
no gaping hole
top dressing only
like soothing words
over an old scar

no need to dig twice
from here to there
there to here
too much ground to cover
filling a hole

and then there is the real reason
resurfacing
black dirt over sour soil
layers of mistakes buried
old bulbs naturalizing
forgotten
tiny corms forming
like a million forgiving eyes

—*Dorothy Mahoney*

Finding Marshfield Woods

We thought the woods in question
might be near the acreage
we had bought, just lately,
on McCormick Road.
And so we travelled along
a gravelled concession,
each side buffered by winter fields
recumbent under snow.

We commented that the rural scene
had so far still survived
the encroaching boundaries
of small towns.
The landfill,
disguised as a hill,
innocuous, white, and clean,
slumbered in the distance.

We saw, startled then,
two hesitant deer
as they approached the road,
and crossed before our slowing truck.
Now foundering in the drifted ditch,
then recovering their footing on the
outstretched field, they fled
across the still-life landscape.

We followed them with our gaze
as they bounded through
the waning daylight towards
a softly darkening wood-lot.
And for a moment sharing
their heaving bodies, their pounding hearts,
we were there too: reaching the woods,
imagining our relief, our sanctuary.

We sat wondering in a shared
bond of silence, until, moving
a little up the road,
we knew.
This was the Marshfield Wood.
For, through the close of light,
the loggers were leaving the
fresh cut fairways through the trees.

—*Marie Groundwater*

Squirters

maple keys stuck in the grass
fan tails up
like fish feeding
like pins stuck there
for safe keeping
like a crazy grid
of how many maples
could grow
and a plot of where
like dried wings
driven downward
like fingers on a keyboard
a dervish of falling words
clicking

—*Dorothy Mahoney*

Burden

so many nests concealed
yet shards of blue
seized in the grass
mark a robin's delay
there is no holding on
to even this light burden

how cumbersome fingers
when birds can weave a nest
of spider silk and moss
twine grass and twigs
together
to cup a clutch
between the prongs
of honeysuckle bush

to woo with songs
thread through the
thick of evergreen and
trilled through thickets
of blooming elderberry
the hide and seek of wings
through spring-embellished
leaves

we have no wings
will never light upon a branch
or flee in flight
from looming shadows

sigh and sit heavy
while birds sing

—*Dorothy Mahoney*

Moonlight Sonatas

In my childhood you were
a green-cheese moon,
gibbous in the sky;
a man-in-the-moon,
dimpled and dreamy;
a monster moon between the buildings,
threatening the city street;
a neverland moon to the place
of sleeping time.

And as I grew to love you were
a harvest moon
silkening the cornfields;
a highwayman moon
roving country roads;
a paper moon,
translucent
as my heart.

And as I held my child you were
a rocking moon of lullabies,
a cat and the fiddle moon,
a winken, blinken and nod moon
sailing the scudding clouds,
companion of the small hours.

And as I grow to age you are
the moon of tides, exposing
the private places beneath
the heaving waves,
ravishing the briny deep.
You are
the lunatic moon,
laughing and beckoning.

—*Marie Groundwater*

Potato Soup

this is the recipe I seldom find
when the potatoes are new
instead the paper bag
is like a lunch
forgotten under the stairs
holds small shriveled
potatoes masquerading
as large walnuts
shoots like royal scepters
of velvet purple
with fine white filigree
command attention
centres soft white
an ache of human age

this is when I must run
into the rain or snow
to thyme in the garden
hardened stems hiding
tiny green leaves close to the ground
I inhale thyme on my fingertips
before the onion's peeled
before the peeling of all things
soup-bound
before enough small potatoes
become five medium
before the bag is empty

I study the recipe again
a calendar page of nine years ago
January
a hearty soup
made with baking potatoes
seasoned to taste

—Dorothy Mahoney

Barberry Bushes

as they grow fiercer
the barberry bushes
are a bane to the mailman
the child unsteady on bicycle
the young girl walking
barefooted
thorn-stickled stems
like fine barbed wire
conspire against the
gardener's hands
dive deep into
fingertips
abruptly sensitive to touch

thick stems
bright yellow at the core
threaten like medieval
weaponry
this is the barrier
grown round fairy-tale
castles under spell
there is no rescue
no birds nest here
although berries
might tempt some
here is a bouquet
for an enemy
spiny stems
and purple leaves
like taunting words
best from a distance

banned
it harbours rust
endangers fields of wheat

and yet we let the bushes live
storm them twice a year
conspire to uproot them
no hero willing for the war

—*Dorothy Mahoney*

October Moment

The drizzling wind
spat
a thousand yellow leaves
against my car
which waited,
waxed,
like some art-crafted tree
of veined mosaic.
So strange
to see it growing there,
beside the curb...
then stranger still to sit
within this glass tree-house,
child-eyed,
not turning the key
yet.

—*Marie Groundwater*

Far from the Stars

Sitting on the back porch step
Pen in hand, teacup at my side
I prepare to write a poem about stars
I find a new page in my notebook, try to concentrate
But a small brown toad hops across my foot
And the steam rises fragrant
From my ginger tea

Above my head, the lilac blooms have
Tiny flowers that look like stars
This dawn, their heady sweetness drifted
Through our open bedroom window

I put my mind on a NASA bulletin
That claims the universe is filled with rhythms like
The sounds made by breath in a flute
Then I hear scales floating from the house across the fence
And am back in time
Hearing once again those childish practice notes
And the music of the spheres grows faint again

—Lenore Langs

On Butterfly Wings

If I tell you why I came back
to live in the country, perhaps
you won't understand: surely
I knew there would be
bee hives in the attic,
horse flies, eyes leaden,
buzzing in the garage,
crickets catapulting through
each opened door, and
a huge spider in my mailbox
whenever I reached in.
In the night, the scurrying
of mice would keep me awake
and sometimes, through the dark,
the howling of coyotes and
the screech of – something...

But then, there have been
deer in the early morning fog,
hawks soaring sentinel over the woods,
funny fat toads in the flower beds
and kittens scrambling over straw bales.
I have counted seven rabbits in the
kitchen garden, and oh
when damp fields brought
spring through the windows with
an orchestra of frogs,
I have marvelled at the perseverance
and profusion of life.

Just lately, when all the purple hedges
hung with white berries,
and sumacs blazed,
I saw the last butterfly
rising repeatedly
from the grasses, ever southward
into a raw October wind and
she too knows the pain and
the power, that draw her home.

—*Marie Groundwater*

Cat Napped

Flaked out in the flower bed
Thomas sleeps
amid the frosted petals
of snapdragons,
the purple alyssum
and thick poppy greens
that grow out of season,
– a silent, private jungle
lined by garden stones
and crisp, fallen leaves,
his pupils cracked
like black crevices of earth,
his tiger-stripes curled –
clinging to the arms of sun,
heavy in the lazy breath
of November's sweet day.

—*Karen P. Ouellette*

Through winter window
snow soft-falling curtains all,
even that bright star

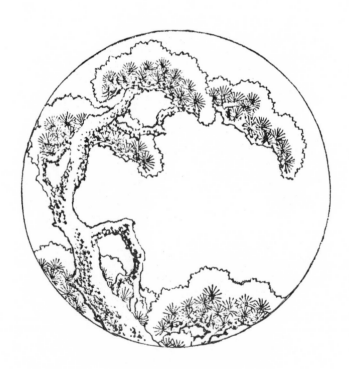

Black Dog

The friend who used to say
this too shall pass away
has been dead for twenty years

When he came ashore
during the war
there were always
celebrations
drinks and long talks
in wardrooms   in hotels
wherever we could meet
As the night wore on
"Down, Boy!" he would shout
"Down, Boy!"

I still hear the black dog
of his drunken imagination
barking at my heart

—*Leila Pepper*

Sunday Afternoon Outing

there are sandwiches
plums and the promise of cookies
maybe chocolate wrapped in purple foil
we sit cramped in the small car
our legs touching
our small feet in sandals
dangle tap the seats in front
we are smiling
in our bathing suits
towels in the trunk
badminton rackets
an old yellow bedspread
a beachball that needs air
we are hot
hold to the promise of water
we have pails to fill with stones and shells
there will be time to draw pictures in the sand
posing for the camera
squinting

it looks like a painting
the sky is blue
the lake stretches for miles
the beach crowded
no one is in the water
we can't get out of the car
a small boy just drowned
no one wants to swim
no one feels like talking

—*Dorothy Mahoney*

Mariposa Nocturna

Suddenly last night
into my closed October room
a white moth flew
beating frantically
against the light

I remembered then
the mariposa blanca
omen of impending death

Today I learned
my nephew has bone cancer
discovered too late
and a Spanish folk tale
becomes reality

　　　　—Leila Pepper

Arts and Crafts

neat needlework
tidy pieces snipped out
small stitches drawing up
the gashes

the pieces of lung
the careful peeling
of a smooth round tumour
attacking the heart

each time the bone snips
the open ribs
a little more chemo
to ensure the cure

—*Lenore Langs*

Continuity

A dizzy head
spins me tonight
whirls my thoughts
like autumn leaves
mixing all my days
I am tired   yet
wakeful and confused
I see faces I once knew
wonderfully unchanged
still so young
I half-believe
the phone will ring and
I will hear their voices
answering questions
I still ask
whose arms do I desire
whose absence
brings most pain?

—*Leila Pepper*

Church-Going

Voices rise around me
random as thistledown
floating on summer air
today the ancient words
we say together
seem fragile and fleeting
like my scattered thoughts
tossed here and there
What if this were
the last time ever
that I sit in
this familiar place
this well-worn pew
kneeling to pray in words
echoing from my childhood?
I used to wonder
in moments of great joy
if this could be
the last time for love
the last time ever
we would lie together
what mercy   what blessing
not to know!

—*Leila Pepper*

44

Sandstorms

My desert is woven
by whimsical cacti,
a kaleidoscope of flowers
the hovering cliffs & chasms
of Sonoran land
where peaceful people
worship in their own way
and wild creatures roam.

But the soul of this desert
is lined in gun-metal grey,
entangled by threats of perennial war
like the sandstorms
that sweep early spring
into wailing walls of wind.

I want to remember
the wings, the harmony
of my hued desert
the fluttering, great-horned owl,
the hum of tiny birds
framing homes,

or the funny long legged roadrunner
as he raced through sand
to a sudden halt
cooing curious at me...

But today, I can only hear
the children screaming
scattering like broken birds,
sounds of shrapnel,
of wingless weapons
streaming through the haze.

—*Karen P. Ouellette*

45

R.E.M. Sleep

The dust of the
Afghani desert
blows through
Manhattan;
veiling the women,
changing the men
into grey warriors
scaling a
rugged terrain.
This is a
bitter landscape
of tortured
metal and mortar,
torn paper
and torn limbs.
Sirens keening
through the nights
disturb our dreams.
From this
apocalyptic nightmare
we have awakened,
and now
we dare not
sleep again.

—*Marie Groundwater*

Your eyes clear water:
no warning winter's coming
would turn them to ice

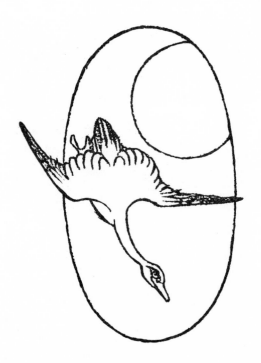

Memory

a small wind comes
to rough my pool of quiet
agitating memories submerged
as pebbles under water
this is no storm
to violate the mind
but a slow stirring of
what used to be
too many years of practice
have worked upon these stones
shining them to smoothness
rubbing away sharp edges of hurt
only the slow waterfall of memory
drips down and with the wind
brings faint shadows
echoes   half pleasure and half pain
I drift on the water
and remember in a drowsy dream
spent yesterdays

—*Leila Pepper*

Coldframe

how easily the old sandbox
could become a coldframe

beneath the cover
in damp sand
plastic shovels
and rusted trucks
are buried
only beetles tunnel there
where excavations once
were daily
where water flooded
through canals
and armies battled
across stick bridges
so many uses for stones
where now dried leaves
have filigreed
and spider eggs
like wadded cotton
hang in looping webs
across corners

where are the little fingers
little toes
that found such glee in sand
how it filled pockets
stuck wet to hair and lined
creases and folds
ears and elbows
children of sand
how quickly you vanished

—*Dorothy Mahoney*

Ursuline Academy

Upstairs at the music school
Sister is waiting
beside an old upright
festooned with trailing plants.
There is a shaded window
held open by a block of wood and she
is watching pigeons on the rooftop.
When she hears the child's footsteps
on the polished stair she rises
and stepping soundlessly
across whitened hardwood to the door
opens it before the knock.
Time is a signature behind a bar line.

—*Marie Groundwater*

Summer 1944

goldfish circling in their bowl
on the wide window sill

grandma slicing apples thin
hands whitened flour cascading
from the big bin
in the cupboard

gingham checkered oilcloth
soup clotted with barley
buttered biscuits

shrilling of the noon whistle
grandpa washing in the metal basin
at the kitchen sink

there was a radio
i stopped my ears
to rapid talk of
casualties

—*Lenore Langs*

The Apple Trees

We gathered early that spring
while my father planted apple trees
four young saplings. One, he said,
digging deep into the rich black earth,
for each of you. Mine to cherish
was near the shadowy grape arbour
and it grew tall over the summer.
I dreamed always of big red apples,
apples I would eat that coming fall
for six is an impatient wilful age.
The trees flourished a few years
then one by one in spite of watering
and loving care, withered and died
sapped by some slow and secret blight.
Four separate dreams died with them.
Long after where the trees had stood
I could see them still. Even now
when I dream of my dead father
they are full-bearing, heavy with fruit.

—*Leila Pepper*

Déjà Vu

the old woman watches rainbows
dancing on the carpet
cast by the prism
in the window

remembers

light glancing from a crystal punch bowl
falling in coloured diamonds on
her satin gown

—*Lenore Langs*

Clearing Out

in the basement, sealers
a hundred or more
holding her mustard pickles, chili sauce
black-currant jam

in the upstairs closet, winter coats
the good grey wool
with the persian-lamb collar
the bulky quilted blue
for everyday

in the dresser, boxes
income tax receipts, warranties
brittle clippings
yellowed birth
and death
notices
snaps of people
so long dead
he can't recall
which fading name
written on the back
belongs to
what face

—*Lenore Langs*

55

Painting the Shed Trim
Clayton Lake

I am painting the shed trim
Clayton Lake
a green-blue
like northern lakes
reflecting pine and cedar
my elbow besmirched with blue
my eyes wary of bumblebees
that fly into one corner
and disappear into wood
the ladder tenses
with my weight
and I lean to push the brush
further

behind the shed
a rotting stump has bloomed
ecru-shelves
sunlight filters through
the maple tree
somewhere a woodpecker
is drumming

there's an echo
of children
laughing as they walk
down to a lake
their shoulders slung
with bright towels
their bare feet eager for sand

I brush pine needles
from the shed roof
finish the fourth side
close the ladder
hammer the paint lid
feel the splashes
of *Clayton Lake*
dry on my skin

—*Dorothy Mahoney*

The Old Park Homestead

It always seems to be
the hottest day of summer
August sweating in the fever
of last hours
when I drive out along
the lakeshore road
to find my blueberries.
And always
in my mind
grows the same fear
of no fruit left all
picked and gone and
someone else's freezer
full and breathing with
misted berries,
me too late-
yet even in my haste
I cannot pass the gate
of John Park's farm,
restored for public view.

I walk the path
up by the pumpkin vines
and past the waiting barn
smothering
as one swimming
in the heavy air
borne up to gasp the
coolness of the
old white house
as still it stands between
the earth and sky
on the green shoulder
of an Erie bluff.

Inside again,
the other days are mine;
the smell of bread,
the laughter of their play –
I know the musty rooms,
they smell of summertime-
roses and whispered days.
How cold the year has turned
upon the stair,
the winds of Erie breathing
all about their beds,
the coughing and crying
keeping me from
my sweet blueberries.

—*Marie Groundwater*

59

Rosewood Columns –
Fisher Mansion, Detroit

when a Florentine craftsman
begins to carve
these giant trees
William Shakespeare is re-inventing
the English language

the fingers of the artisan
feel their way
over the silky wood
clusters of grapes and vine leaves emerging
reproducing the picture in his mind's eye
the pillars
in Solomon's temple.

a Teutonic conqueror
laying waste an Italian town
sees the pillars
carries them off to grace
his castled fortress

and now they support
this Detroit ceiling

I stroke
the blackened rosewood
polished by caressing hands
for a dozen generations
and think

of Solomon
and Shakespeare
unknown artisan
Teutonic conqueror
and carved grapes and leaves
surviving

—*Lenore Langs*

In Siletto's Garden

We were two little girls
running between long rows of raspberry canes,
tiptoeing then over patches of strawberries
hidden beneath their jealous leaves.
Waist-high in green where rhubarb stalks
thrust thickly through the soil
and hoisted giant leaves, we broke them,
tearing down the fruity strands,
sucking the sour juice and laughing
at our puckered faces.
When the sky grumbled and heavy raindrops fell
we ran shrieking through the uncut grass,
our small hands grasping those ribbed stems,
the floppy leaves umbrellas till we reached
the shelter of the greenhouse;
Kathleen and I – so young,

—*Marie Groundwater*

Is it drops of rain
falling softly outside? No!
My Grand-daughter's tears

For My Sister

It is the familiar we cling to
not high events or travel
but the every-day of life
my cat on the bed beside me
the smell of coffee drifting up
that picture slightly crooked on
the wall above my cluttered desk
my books   dishes my mother used
dusty flowers mirrored in the hall
today from my window I can see
in the snow-covered garden
small birds seeking crumbs
these are things we know   and
long to keep   the reality
of letters from my sister
her voice on the phone
the memories we share
she   to be still in my world

—Leila Pepper

My Father Seemed...

My father seemed much too large
to write about and
confine to lines
stained fingers gold ring flying
over the worn piano keys
missing the notes of the marches
banging out the war songs
chipping the lettering on the lid
sweating
with his sleeves rolled up
mashing the clapshot
spooning mouthfuls of burnt custard
from the little pot
tossing pickled onions
to the old dog that drooled
on his trouser leg
under the table
laughing
fairly choking on his tea
telling stories
as he ran again
through all the back streets
of the sea-walled town
boys full of mischief
setting lit rafts of paper
floating along the burn
beneath the privies
when the old lads had gone in
and then
another and another
"I mind fine the time..."

after supper
always sitting in his suit
cross-legged in an easy chair
smiling at me when I pushed
up under his paper
taking the pens from his pocket
so I could lean against his heart.

—*Marie Groundwater*

All The Pretty Dresses

You said I was beautiful –
bright like the morning sun,
proudly sent me off
to my first day of school
wearing a wool-plaid skirt
of black & red pleats
with matching straps
and frilly-white blouse.

And when the teacher
announced that she would pick
the prettiest,
best dressed girls of the class,
I gladly waited,
my name never called
– heart running home to you.

Weeks later we crossed
the border to shop at Hudsons,
my six year old eyes
soon fixed on the slim,
mascara-lashed mannequins
that modeled Detroit's
latest dresses.

"When I grow up
I want to be a mannequin," I said,
but you led me away
from the stiff icons of beauty
with a mother's hand...

As days weave new dawns,
I wear a black & red
September-gown –
recalling your vision,
your life-long words
that taught me
how to walk beautiful
down my own runway of dreams.

—*Karen P. Ouellette*

Ralph's Dance

In this sunless place
the doctors say
you are anti-social –
violent;
so why are you
slow dancing with me?

Why do you nuzzle
your gentle head
against my cheek;
blow sweet kisses
through my hair
tangled by a brother's
special love?

And why do we sway
amid a friendly crowd
to songs warm
like evening-breeze
where laughter reigns
for a spell
above the fear
of tomorrow's pain?

They say you cannot
feel the measure of time,
so why do I see tears
move your midnight eyes;
feel your feet stepping
soft with mine?

—*Karen P. Ouellette*

Needle and Trowel

I

She pulls delicate wefts
past rows
of perennial seeds
sown to create
a garden-cloth,
her fingers working long –
callused from needle
and trowel,

each promised sprout
like an April-child
growing beneath her hands
– a hued tapestry
harvested
by mother's love.

II

In the unheated attic
I watch her sew
my new tweed coat
on an old treadle machine,
her body sweatered,
the scent of an Easter lily
trailing up the stairwell
on this damp March day,

and I can see the morning sun
play upon her busy face.

III

We are siblings
in pajamas
ordered to pick raspberries
for breakfast,
dodging mosquitoes
and yellow jackets,
our fingers stippled red
our bodies wiry
braiding
through the brambles
like tanned hunters,
laughing, bickering –
hungry for the day.

IV

With her hand guiding mine
we begin to tack rose appliques
to the small collar
of my red corduroy dress
– stitches of spring.

V

She places canning jars
over cut roses
like small glass tents
planted in September's dawn;
waters unseen roots
until frost creeps in,
her blossoms fragile
as fine embroidery
raised from crystal-cloth

and every spring
her garden petalled-pink.

VI

From the afternoon light
where philodendron
climbs round a wooden sill,
she patterns
my first dance costume
of delphinium-blue,
the chiffon
pinned, basted
as I stand proud
on the stage
of a grey kitchen chair,
an untrained dancer –
a little girl
waiting for the glitter,
her sequins covering me
with dreams come true.

VII

How the mock orange
catches summer's breeze
with perfumed threads
as we rest like fledglings
beneath the green cutwork
of pines,
the day overcast,
mom and Aunt Marie
bending,
clipping honeysuckle,
the weeds and burdock
that border home,
our mulberry-stained –
pool-wet feet
warming
on a rose-brick floor.

73

VIII

Listen to my heart;
it is a drum beating
a lover's song
a dancer's rhythm
pulling me toward
his waiting eyes,
mother of pearl
strung by years
of family love
warm upon my skin,
blushing-red roses
gathered
like petalled-notes
folded long
upon my wedding gown.

IX

Watch her work
June's fertile soil
with shovel and rake,
or the fine filigree
of my maternity blouses –
of infant things,
father's old christening
gown waiting
to be pressed.

See the years
light upon her face
like golden springs
that hold the wonder
of baby's breath,
the First Communion dress
finished white and long
– silverlace vine.

X

Today she plaits
August roses
and Queen Anne's Lace
through layers of ivory mesh,
the rhythm of scissors
cutting across a tiled floor,
the chatter of women –
of busy hands sewing
gathering

grand-daughter's wedding veil
trailing down an aisle
of love.

XI

When I inhale the scent
of fresh cut grass
we are home again
planting rainbow-tulips
threaded like drawnwork
over time's distant land
where snow angels
stay stitched
upon my heart.

When I listen
to the trill of sparrows
we sing again of spring,
of feet waltzing
love's garden maze
– our colours lush
and interwoven.

—*Karen P. Ouellette*

Resurrection

I planted the flowering quince
The spring my mother died
This June decided to move it
To a different part of the garden
Where it would have more sun
And be less buffeted by winter storms

I dug out as much of the root as I could –
The root ball was much too heavy to lift
So I dragged the bush to the deep hole
I had prepared for it

Tamped firmly into the new spot
Top-dressed with peat moss and watered in
The bush looked healthy
For three days
Then all the leaves began to brown and crispen
And my neighbour said
"Well, I guess your plant died after all."

I left it there

Last week on the tip of one top branch
A coppery leaf unfurled
This morning, one whole branch
Opened leaves to the sky

—*Lenore Langs*

Trust

I finger pewter-coloured leaves
velvety plants descended from seeds
my grandfather gave me for my first garden

bright fuschia blooms on tall stems
and anything in that shade
reminds me of them and him

we sit at the scrubbed kitchen table
and he spins his stories and he lives
in my mind these past thirty years

once he drove the cream wagon
from house to house pouring foaming milk
from the big can into customers' jugs

the train took the young men west
for the harvest and he lives upstairs
in my mind and I remember

the warm quarter pressed into my palm
at the end of the holiday before
we climbed into the car and waved

at seventy-five he worked a full shift
at the knitting mill in Guelph
the only one who could coax the old machines to life

—*Lenore Langs*

Garden Window

Sometimes we look
through life's window
with different views;
sometimes cloudbursts
bring me fuschia
and flowering words
leaving you
a palette of tears.

Today you throw away
your African violets
fearing they will not bloom –
unable to paint the beauty
of their lush-leaf faces
or sense the presence
of incipient-blue.

Perhaps at times you feel
like a seedling lost
in Van Gogh's spring,
a restless artist
trying to sketch
what you have not touched
but long to know.

And so I remain
your poet-gardener
loving in all storms;
from this glass canvas
I write down our wild violets,
the remembered *Irises*
and *Fourteen Sunflowers*
for you to brush
against your fallen greys.

—*Karen P. Ouellette*

Lear At Stratford

"So we'll live,
and pray, and sing, and tell old tales,
and laugh at gilded butterflies..."
        —Shakespeare, King Lear

Lear at Stratford meant a long drive
up a November highway
leafy with rain,
and only my younger brother
came with me in the car.

If anything, a stormy night was right – for Lear.
We chatted on about the play:
the moors, the madness, things that people say
...or don't, inside a family.

We seemed easy together, there alone
as the road wore on, turning back our minds
to times when we were both at home;
his small adventures as a boy.

I hadn't known, 'til then,
how much our hurt and loss
had made a silence of those years
before our father died – the kitchen table times –
a silence of my brother's childhood.
How eager he had been to hear
the stories I had shut away like a keepsake box.

Beside me, in the dark, he had
a man's voice that I had heard before:
soft cadences and laughter.
I knew the play, and knew Cordelia now,
her love more ponderous than her tongue.

    —Marie Groundwater

The Caterpillar

does not know
the sky
but crawls labouriously
on many legs,
bound to branch and twig.

Fanned by a leafy breeze
it is content to
feel its way along,
worm-like and hairy,
consuming without care.

It does not question the need
for the deep sleep that comes,
the chrysalis closed
within the brittle cocoon,
calm and quiet and strange.

Soon, it will stir, emerge,
stretch unaccustomed wings;
and tinctured, transparent,
aerial now...it rises
to inhabit the unfettered air.

—*Marie Groundwater*

Marie Groundwater (Pottle) was born in the Orkney Islands, Scotland, and came to Canada as a child. She now lives on the shore of Lake Erie in a rural farming community near Harrow, Ontario. Through her years of teaching and her work in dramatic arts with young people, Marie hopes she has passed on her own love of literature and writing. Her work has been published in *2001: A Space Anthology*, *Generation*, *Vintage '93*, and *Wayzgoose*.

Lenore Langs teaches creative writing at the University of Windsor and is co-publisher/editor (with Laurie Smith) of Cranberry Tree Press. With Adele Wiseman, she established the Wayzgoose interuniversity reading series, which involved schools in Michigan and Ontario, and which ran for ten years. Lenore's work has been published in literary journals and anthologies in Canada and the United States.

Dorothy Mahoney teaches at Essex District High School. She has two books of poetry published by Black Moss Press.

Karen P. Ouellette's poetry is influenced by her work with the handicapped and by years of ballet studies. Twice a finalist for the C.P.A. poetry competition, she is published in literary journals and anthologies, including *Kaleidoscope*, *Seeds*, *Whetstone*, and most recently, *Body Language: A Head-to-Toe Anthology* (Black Moss Press), and *2003: Tea for Three* (Cranberry Tree Press). Karen has read her poems on CBC radio and at venues throughout Ontario and Michigan.

Leila Pepper has been a writer since childhood. Returning to her studies at sixty, she earned her Master's Degree in English Literature and Creative Writing at the University of Windsor under the tutelage of Alistair MacLeod and W.O. Mitchell. She has published four books of poetry (Black Moss Press), and her poems have been printed in many magazines, including *Canadian Poetry Magazine*, *The Fiddlehead*, and the Detroit Women Writers' Anthology. As well, she has read her poetry at Harbourfront and The Detroit Institute of Arts. In 1997, Leila was awarded the Windsor Mayor's Award for Literary Excellence.

In Acknowledgement

Some of these poems have appeared in the following literary periodicals and anthologies: *2001: A Space Anthology* (Cranberry Tree Press); Canadian Poetry Association anthologies; *Generation*; *Open Windows 3* (Hidden Brook Press); *Qwerty; Rattle; Of Rocks and Rhythm 2003* (Ontario Poetry Society); *Vintage '96* (League of Canadian Poets); *Wayzgoose* Anthologies; *Windsor Review*.

Some of Dorothy Mahoney's poems have appeared in *Returning to the Point* (Black Moss Press).

Some of Leila Pepper's poems have appeared in her books *Caught in Amber, The Hidden World, Love Poems For Several Men,* and *In War With Time* (Black Moss Press).

CRANBERRY TREE PRESS

The book was typeset in Sabon with titles in ITC Eras.
Sabon was designed by Jan Tschichold in 1964.
The roman is based on designs by Claude Garamond,
and the italic on designs of Robert Granjon.
ITC Eras was designed in 1976 by
Albert Boton and Albert Hollenstein.

Layout and design of this book was by David Langs.

The book was printed and bound by AGMV Marquis,
Quebec, Canada.